GIRAFFES

by Liza Jacobs

BLACKBIRCH®
PRESS

THOMSON

GALE

San Diego • Detroit • New York • San Francisco • Cleveland • New Haven, Conn. • Waterville, Maine • London • Munich

For more information, contact
The Gale Group, Inc.
27500 Drake Rd.
Farmington Hills, MI 48331-3535
Or you can visit our Internet site at http://www.gale.com

Photographs © 1990 by Chang Yi-Wen

Cover Photograph © PhotoDisc

Illustration by Yan Kai-Xin

© 1990 by Chin-Chin Publications Ltd.

No. 274-1, Sec.1 Ho-Ping E. Rd., Taipei, Taiwan, R.O.C.
Tel: 886-2-2363-3486 Fax: 886-2-2363-6081

LIBRARY OF CONGRESS CATALOGING-IN-PUBLICATION DATA

Jacobs, Liza.
  Giraffes / by Liza Jacobs.
    p. cm. — (Wild wild world)
  Summary: An introduction to the animal that has a long tongue, likes to eat leaves, and lives in a small group.
  Includes bibliographical references.
  ISBN 1-4103-0076-5 (hardback : alk. paper)
  1. Giraffe—Juvenile literature. [1. Giraffe.] I. Title. II. Series.

QL737.U56L8 2003
599.638—dc21   2002152041

Printed in Taiwan
10 9 8 7 6 5 4 3 2 1

Table of Contents

Giraffe Facts

Giraffes are the tallest land animals.

An adult giraffe can be up to 19 feet tall.

They are heavy animals that weigh between 1,500 and 4,200 pounds.

Giraffes have manes of stiff hair running down their backs.

They have short fur with brownish and whitish markings.

No two giraffes look exactly alike.

Each giraffe has its own unique pattern of markings on its fur.

Giraffes also have tails up to 3 feet long.

The Giraffe Body

Giraffes love to eat leaves from trees.

Their long necks help them reach the treetops.

A giraffe's neck can be more than 5 feet long!

A giraffe's long legs are very strong.

To eat ground plants and drink water, giraffes have to bend over very far.

They spread their front legs wide and lean their necks way down to ground.

7

Giraffe Senses

Giraffe horns are covered with skin and fur. They protect a giraffe's head.

A male giraffe's horns are longer than a female's.

Giraffes have large eyes and keen eyesight. Long eyelashes protect their eyes from dust and wind. Hair in their ears help to protect in the same way.

Giraffes also have a good sense of smell. And they can open and shut their nostrils to keep out dirt.

Long lashes protect against sand and dirt.

Hairs in the ears help to filter out dirt.

Nostrils can open and shut.

A Long, Long Tongue

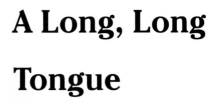

Giraffes have very long tongues. A giraffe's tongue is 18 to 20 inches long!

Giraffes use their long tongues to grab leaves from trees.

They can reach into small spaces to grasp what they need.

A giraffe's tongue is tough and is not bothered by prickly leaves or rough branches.

Giraffe Food

Giraffes love to eat leaves.

Their upper lips are very strong and help them pull leaves off trees.

In places where there are not enough trees, giraffes also eat grasses and herbs.

In zoos, giraffes are often fed greens, corn, apples, and carrots.

Giraffes can eat 70 to 100 pounds of leaves in a day. They spend almost half their day eating!

Digesting and Resting

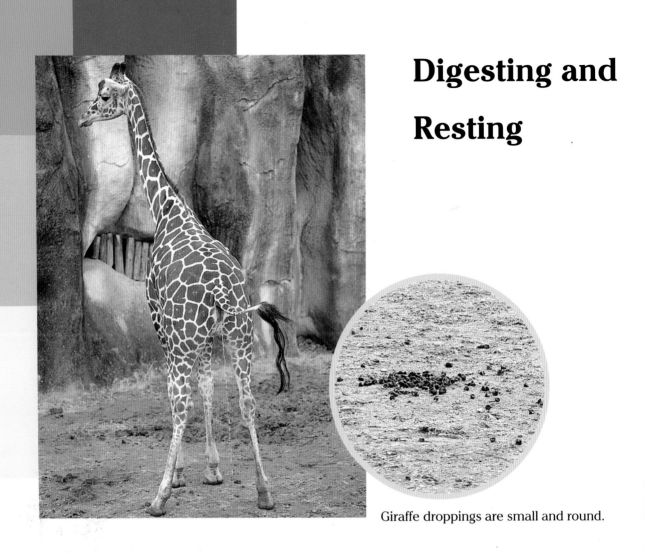

Giraffe droppings are small and round.

To pee, a giraffe lifts its tail and widens its back legs.

Its poop   or droppings   falls to the ground.

In the wild, giraffes only sleep a few hours each night.

They often sleep standing up. When they do lie down, they get up from time to time. This helps keep them safe from lion attacks. Lions are their main enemies.

Giraffes also sleep with their legs tucked under their bodies and their necks upright.

They may rest their heads on their bodies, but just for a few minutes at time.

Giraffe Groups

Giraffes are gentle animals that live in small groups.

Sometimes several small groups travel together in large herds.

Giraffes standing together often turn their heads to look different ways. This lets the group see any animals coming near.

A male giraffe is called a bull. A female is called a cow.

Baby Giraffes

A baby giraffe is called a calf.

A mother giraffe is pregnant for about 15 months.

She gives birth to her baby while standing up.

A calf weights about 100 pounds at birth. It stands about 6 feet tall.

Baby giraffes drink their mother's milk for 12 to 15 months.

The knobs of a baby giraffe are smaller and softer than adult giraffe horns.

A baby giraffe is born with horns.

Baby giraffes can walk just a few minutes after birth.

Giraffes walk slowly. But they can also run very fast   up to 35 miles per hour!

By the time it is 5 years old, a young giraffe will reach its adult height.

Baby giraffes like to play. They will follow and chase after their mother.

Peaceful Creatures

Mother giraffes look after their babies and protect them.

They like to nuzzle their babies. A mother giraffe will wrap her neck around her baby to comfort it.

Giraffes are peaceful creatures that take good care of each other.

For More Information

Jango-Cohen, Judith. *Giraffes*. Tarrytown, NY: Benchmark Books, 2001.

Kalman, Bobbie.*Giraffes*. New York: Crabtree, 1997.

Schaefer, Lola. *Giraffes: Long-Necked Leaf Eaters*. Mankato, MN: Bridgestone Books, 2001.

Glossary

bull a male giraffe

calf a baby giraffe

cow a female giraffe

herd a group of giraffes